Introduction to

Harnessing Your
Emotions

Andrew Wommack

© Copyright 2025 – Andrew Wommack

Printed in the United States of America. All rights reserved. No portion of this book may be reproduced, stored in a retrieval system, or transmitted in any form or by any means—electronic, mechanical, photocopy, recording, scanning, or other—except for brief quotations in critical reviews or articles, without the prior written permission of the publisher.

Unless otherwise indicated, all Scripture quotations are taken from the King James Version® of the Bible. Copyright © by the British Crown. Public domain.

Scripture quotations marked (NIV) are taken from the Holy Bible, New International Version®, NIV®. Copyright © 1973, 1978, 1984, 2011 by Biblica, Inc.™ Used by permission of Zondervan. All rights reserved worldwide. www.zondervan.com The "NIV" and "New International Version" are trademarks registered in the United States Patent and Trademark Office by Biblica, Inc.™

Scripture quotations marked (AMP) are taken from the Amplified Bible, Copyright © 2015 by The Lockman Foundation. Used by permission.

Published by Andrew Wommack Ministries, Inc.
Woodland Park, CO 80863

ISBN 13 TP: ISBN: 978-1-59548-764-3

For Worldwide Distribution, Printed in the USA

1 2 3 4 5 6 / 28 27 26 25

Contents

Introduction 1
Psychology vs. Christianity 3
Be Spiritually Minded 5
You Get to Choose 8
The Trap of Self-Esteem 9
Living in Christ-Esteem 13
Be Better, Not Bitter 15
Selfless Perspective 18
Be Dependent on God 20
Sin Is Conceived 22
Let Not Your Heart Be Troubled 24
Bringing Power Under Authority 26
Exercising Control 28
A Merry Heart Does Good 30
How Do You See Yourself? 32
Change Your Thinking 34
Renew Your Mind 36
Our Light Afflictions 38
Rejoice in the Lord 40
Bless the Lord at All Times 42
You Can Control Your Emotions 44
Conclusion 47
Receive Jesus As a Savior 51
Receive the Holy Spirit 53

Would you like to get more out of this teaching?

Scan the QR code to access this teaching in video or audio formats to help you dive even deeper as you study.

Accessing the teaching this way will help you get even more out of this booklet.

awmi.net/browse

Introduction

Everybody has emotions. They are one of the spices of life. But sadly, most people struggle with their feelings. They are not in control of their emotions; their emotions are in control of them. That is not how things ought to be according to the Word of God.

Riding a horse is one of the great pleasures I've had in life, but there's nothing worse than riding a horse that is totally out of control. Likewise, emotions add joy to life when they are serving us, but when our emotions control us, watch out. We are headed for a fall.

I'm going to be sharing some things with you that have the potential to transform your life. Learning to harness your emotions is one of the keys to walking with the Lord and living an effective Christian life.

Most people will agree that emotions are important and that nobody truly wants to be sad, bothered, fearful, or negative. But there are a lot of people who—even though they desire to be positive and joyful—don't take any responsibility for their emotions. They don't believe they can control how they feel.

They'll tell you they act the way they do because of some trauma in their life. They'll say things like, "Well, I just can't help it!" They let their emotions run wild and get out of control. They end up damaging relationships, losing jobs, and experiencing other repercussions. But often these people will not take accountability for their actions or emotions.

Your emotions are not like the caboose of a train that just follows whatever happens in your life. Your emotions are more comparable to the engine. It's what drives things. And you can choose how you want to feel.

Secular psychology has influenced nearly every area of society and, sad to say, it is practically dominant in Christianity today. Psychology excuses behavior, especially emotions, as just reactions to our environment. It treats us like animals that just react to stimuli, saying it's our environment and what people do to us that make us the way we are. That's not what the Bible teaches.

Sure, bad things happen to each of us, and some people have more bad things happen to them than others. That's life in a fallen world. But we aren't just evolved animals. We are people, created in God's image, and we can rejoice in the Lord regardless of what comes our way. Otherwise, the Lord would have been unjust to give us commands like in Psalm 34:1; John 14:1, 16:33; and Philippians 4:4.

Now, I'm not condemning anyone, but people who are emotionally immature forsake the instruction of Scripture for psychology. They're going by the common thinking, priorities, and values of the world—carnal-mindedness—and it's producing death (Rom. 8:6).

The emotional stability of people today is much worse than it was a generation ago. And yet, people should be doing much better. We have so many conveniences that make things easier; productivity has increased. We should be doing better, but we aren't. I believe it is because of psychology, wrong attitudes, and people letting their emotions dominate and control them.

There is a better way to live than letting the things of this world dominate you and letting yourself be controlled by emotions. Once you find out what Scripture says, you'll start living in the fullness of God's goodness and freedom.

Psychology vs. Christianity

Even so every good tree bringeth forth good fruit; but a corrupt tree bringeth forth evil fruit. A good tree cannot bring forth evil fruit, neither can *a corrupt tree bring forth good fruit.*

Matthew 7:17–18

Psychology has its roots in ancient philosophers like Socrates, Aristotle, and Plato. None of these men were worshipers of the true and living God. At best, they believed in a god that was not involved in the affairs of men, and at worst, they worshiped multiple pagan gods.

Modern psychology was brought to the forefront by Sigmund Freud in the late nineteenth century. Freud certainly wasn't a godly man. He was obsessed with sex and linked every problem of man to the sexual drive. This man had some serious problems, and his most devoted followers openly admit that.

The root of psychology is bad, and therefore, the fruit cannot be good. I'm amazed at the acceptance of psychology in our society and especially in the church. There are churches and ministries that have resident psychiatrists on staff. This isn't the approach Jesus took.

I know many Christians are appalled at these statements. Now, I have some friends who are very successful psychologists. They use their position to bring the truths of the Gospel to people who would never come to the church for help. But they will be the first to admit that psychology and Christianity do not offer the same answers to our problems.

Jesus met all the needs of the people through the power of the Holy Spirit, and I believe He intends His church to do the same. They don't have to depart and go to the world to get their emotional needs met. They should bring them to Jesus (Matt. 14:16–18).

Christianity and psychology do have some things in common: They both state that our actions are the product of inner processes. But in describing what those processes are and how to change them, Christianity and psychology take opposite approaches.

Here are four major tenets of psychology I believe are incompatible with biblical Christianity:

1. We are products of our environment.
2. Therefore, we are not responsible or accountable for our actions.
3. This leads us to blame anyone but ourselves for our own actions—a victim mentality.
4. Self-esteem is paramount.

Psychology undermines true Christianity, and these differences need to be pointed out. It has crept into nearly every aspect of our lives, and most of us don't know it. But when you know the truth of God's Word, you'll be set free (John 8:32).

Be Spiritually Minded

For to be carnally minded is death; but to be spiritually minded is life and peace.

Romans 8:6

Our environment does not solely influence who we are. It has some impact, but the Bible teaches us that *our thoughts* primarily control our actions. Notice that carnal-mindedness doesn't just tend toward death — it is death! Proverbs 23:7 says, "For *as he thinketh in his heart, so* is *he.*" And Isaiah 26:3 says the Lord will keep a person in perfect peace if their "*mind* is *stayed* on" Him.

People can't consistently perform differently than the way they think; therefore, we cannot change our actions without changing our thinking. It's not just what we think about that needs changing; we need to change our thinking process. Our emotions are linked directly to how we think.

Everyone has a perception—or image—on the inside of them of what they are like. This image is not necessarily based on facts but on feelings. One negative experience can distort a person's perception of themselves for a lifetime.

For instance, some beautiful people may think of themselves as ugly or undesirable because of unkind words spoken to them as a child. Some who achieve great success still see themselves as failures, which may become a self-fulfilling prophecy. It creates a performance mentality that is unhealthy.

I remember a woman who shared her testimony about always having to be perfect. When she was eight years old, her mother died. Her father—who didn't feel capable of raising his children as a single parent—left her at an orphanage, promising to visit her every Saturday. On Saturday mornings, this girl would wear her very best dress, waiting for her father to arrive. But he never came to visit. She did this every Saturday until she grew up and left the orphanage.

Out of that event in her life, she got the idea that people wouldn't love her unless she was perfect. She was convinced no one would accept her if they saw her real self. This woman developed a performance mentality.

When she got married, she never let her husband see her unless she was perfectly dressed, made up, and composed. Then, one day, they got into an argument. All the pressure this woman put on herself finally caused her to break down. In the middle of that argument, she started to cry, her makeup ran, *and her cover was blown!* She wasn't "Miss Perfect" anymore!

At some point, she finally blurted out, "Fine, divorce me! I don't care!" But instead of storming out, her husband laughed and asked, "Why would I divorce you?" Then she yelled back, "Because now you know what I'm really like!"

Here was someone who seemingly had it all together but had a wrong perspective of herself due to something that happened in the past and the negative thoughts and feelings she developed as a result.

You Get to Choose

I call heaven and earth to record this day against you, that I have set before you life and death, blessing and cursing: therefore choose life, that both thou and thy seed may live.

Deuteronomy 30:19

All of us have had negative experiences. We get to choose whether we become bitter or better as a result of them. For every person who can claim some dysfunctional behavior because of a traumatic experience in their life, there are others who have had similar or worse things happen to them, yet they overcame their circumstances. Why? Because problems do not dictate failure; we have a choice.

God gives us a choice; He doesn't make the choice for us. Other people can't make the choice for us. Not even Satan can make the choice for us! Years ago, the comedian Flip Wilson popularized the phrase "The devil made me do it!" through his television show. It may have been funny to his audience, but in reality, that statement just isn't true. Satan can't do anything without our consent and cooperation. *We* have the responsibility to choose blessing or cursing.

Placing blame on others is denying the real problem, and it will prevent finding a solution. If other people are my problem, I'm in trouble because God did not give me the ability to control other people. But if the problem is within *me*, then there is hope because, through Christ, I can change. This is freedom. Regardless of what others do, I can prosper through Christ.

In contrast, psychology says we prosper through our human strength and that solutions can only come from what's available in our human potential. But that's totally against what the Bible teaches.

Jesus said, *"For without me ye can do nothing"* (John 15:5), and *"Whosoever will come after me, let him deny himself, and take up his cross, and follow me"* (Mark 8:34).

The Lord made us so we could choose our own way. We have that choice. But the best choice a person can make is to say, "Father, I don't trust in myself. I am not self-dependent, self-reliant, or self-sufficient. I need You, Lord. Without You, I can do nothing."

The Trap of Self-Esteem

To a degree, psychology has correctly diagnosed the problem, which, for most individuals, stems from their perceptions, thoughts, and attitudes. Psychologists use terminology such as "self-esteem" or "identity" in relating these truths. However, today's secular wisdom is totally inadequate to help a person change their inner self-image.

The root word of "psychology" is a derivative of the Greek word *psyche*, meaning "soul."[1] Psychology looks no deeper than the soul of man for answers. It totally ignores the spirit realm, which includes our spirits, God's Holy Spirit, and demonic spirits. Psychology tries to bolster your self-esteem by having you focus on the positive things in yourself and minimize the negative attributes. It tries to solve problems from a purely natural, physical standpoint, not from the standpoint of the supernatural ability of God.

The Word of God is full of examples of the influence of God, demons, and our spirits on our actions. Jesus ministered to a man who was driven to live in the tombs and spent his days crying and cutting himself because of the emotional torment caused by demons (Mark 5:1–20). Once Jesus cast out the demons, this man returned to "*his right mind*" and went about sharing the "*great things [Jesus] had done for him.*" That's awesome!

Any answer that doesn't take the spirit realm into account isn't getting to the real root of the problem. Another word for this approach is humanism. In other words, humanists believe we already have all the answers within ourselves, and we don't need God. According to humanistic philosophy, the answer to our problems is not found in the spiritual part of us, but in the mental and emotional part. That is totally wrong.

In the case of the woman who tried to be perfect, psychologists might say that any negative behavior caused by childhood abandonment was not her fault. She could have just stayed bitter and blamed her father or even God for how her life turned out.

They would say her husband should have built up his wife's self-esteem by telling her how great she was, or how perfect she looked. But thankfully, this woman's husband went beyond soulish things and ministered to her condition spiritually. He showed her God's unconditional love instead, and it totally transformed her life.

He said, "I love you the way you are. It doesn't matter what you think you're really like." And it just disarmed this woman. She had never considered that someone could love her regardless of her performance.

This woman's emotions had started to get out of control at a young age. By the time she was an adult, her whole personality had developed around her performance. So, when a crisis hit, she just fell apart like a two-dollar suitcase. Years later, I met this woman when she hosted a television show in the Chicago area, and she and her husband were doing well and were a blessing to others.

Christians should not rely on the positive attributes of their personalities. That is like trying to stop the bleeding from an amputated arm with a Band-Aid; it won't work for long.

Regardless of how successful or talented we are, we will eventually fail. If nothing else, we will get older someday and will not be as productive or beautiful as before. If our self-esteem is rooted in our accomplishments or looks, then it will ultimately fail. All the security we have found in ourselves will then come crashing down around us. You need to come to the end of yourself and find your fulfillment in Jesus.

I know another woman who was repeatedly sexually abused as a child. This led to her having a very promiscuous life well into her forties. Even after her salvation experience, she continued to let herself be abused by men because she felt she couldn't help it. She didn't want that, but it was just who she was.

She was constantly seeking pity from me. I did show compassion to her, but I loved her enough to tell her the truth. Regardless of what was done to her by others, God's grace was greater (Rom. 5:20). She could not only overcome all her sexual desires, but she could live totally free from all the emotional damage attached to her abuse.

She did eventually get free from having sexual relations with men outside of marriage, but she did it through her own willpower, which left her nursing all her old hurts and pains. She was still a victim and not a victor. She approached everything in her life from the soulish realm with a victim mentality. That's not freedom.

Living in Christ-Esteem

Therefore if any man be in Christ, he is a new creature: old things are passed away; behold, all things are become new.

2 Corinthians 5:17

I agree that self-image and self-esteem are important, but it all comes down to which self is being esteemed. It is not our old, carnal self but our new, born-again self that we need to focus on and esteem.

It's not really accurate for Christians to use the term self-esteem. It would be more accurate for us to say "Christ-esteem." As Christians, we shouldn't esteem our old, fleshly, carnal selves; we should esteem our new, born-again selves. When we do that, not only will our actions and emotions be affected, but when we blow it, we won't be surprised and discouraged.

We will recognize that the old fleshly part of us has been allowed to rule. If we are born again, our old man—our old sin nature—is dead and gone (Rom. 6:6). Everything in our spirit is made new (2 Cor. 5:17), but to get the things of God into our souls—where our emotions reside—we need to renew our minds to the Word of God (Rom. 12:2).

If we understand these truths, then when we have negative feelings and emotions, instead of being shocked or thinking,

How could I think such a thing?, we will realize, *Oh, that's just my old flesh, because my new man doesn't think that way.*

When we esteem our new man, we focus on Jesus and esteem Christ in us (Col. 1:27). This makes us aware that we are brand-new spirits. And when we keep ourselves spiritually minded, we can more easily walk according to the spirit and not the flesh. If a person isn't very conscious of who they are spiritually, it's easy for them to slip back into the physical.

I knew a pastor who loved the Lord and saw miracles happen in his ministry. But he became jealous of his wife and her friendship with a coworker. He blew the situation way out of proportion, which led him into an emotional rage. He began thinking negatively and experiencing emotions he should have never entertained. In the process, he got so mad at God that he drove down the street, threw his Bible out the window, and went and did drugs because that's what he did before he was born again. He ended up overdosing and nearly died!

Later, when I went to see him in the psych ward of the hospital, he said, "I thought I was more mature than this. How could a person who loved God, witnessed for Him, and been a pastor do something like this?" I was able to minister to this man that all he did was step outside his born-again spirit and deal with that situation in his old natural self. He had fallen victim to the trap of leaning on himself rather than relying on what Jesus had already done and who he was in his new spirit. He thought he should have been past doing things like he did. But our flesh doesn't improve or mature with time. The victory in the Christian life is living in the spirit and denying the flesh.

It's like a person flying in a plane. They may be 30,000 feet in the air and flying at 500 miles per hour, but it's not them that's doing that. It's the plane, and it's only their position in that plane that enables them to do that. If they step out of the plane, they will sink like a rock. Likewise, the victory in the Christian life is abiding in Jesus. When we step out of who we are in Christ, we fail every time because without Him, we can do nothing (John 5:5).

Be Better, Not Bitter

Most people shift the blame for bad self-esteem or self-image to someone else. It has become popular to blame others for every negative thing in our lives. People say, "I came from a dysfunctional family," "My problems came because I'm part of a minority group," or something similar. It all began when God confronted Adam about his sin, and the man responded, "It's that woman You gave me" (Gen. 3:12). But, as we've seen, other people are not our problem!

Some friends of mine had a daughter who went through some real struggles. She got into drugs and even left home for a time. It broke her parents' hearts.

Finally, her parents submitted her to Christian counseling, but it ended up being more psychological than biblical. The counselors told this girl things like, "The reason this happened was because your parents didn't love you. They were too strict. They didn't allow you to express your own individuality."

These counselors placed the blame for her actions on her parents. Now, I'm not condemning people who seek Christian counseling. But what I am saying is that this couple did more for their daughter than 99.9 percent of kids her age ever experienced. They weren't perfect, but they loved her and did their best. There are millions of kids who had it worse than this girl and didn't rebel.

What I'm saying is that we don't have to just react. We can choose to act in a godly way regardless of what happens to us. God gave us authority over our emotions.

I was raised in a loving family, but my dad died when I was twelve years old, so I grew up without a father. Psychologists would say there's no way I could be normal because I grew up in a single-parent home. Now, like most kids, I was thoughtless and forgetful. There were times when my mother had to correct me. But even when I did wrong, it was not because of an attitude of rebellion.

As they played my dad's favorite song at his funeral, "How Great Thou Art," I thought, *This is weird!* You see, I was told that it was God's will that my father died. In church, I had been taught that God punishes people, He puts sickness on them, and if they didn't measure up to His standard, they could expect the wrath of God.

I could have been bitter or even angry at God, but I did the exact opposite. I remember sitting at that funeral, praying, "God, if You're truly great, reveal Yourself to me. Show me what You want to do with my life."

At just twelve years old, the Lord showed me Psalms 27:10, which says,

When my father and my mother forsake me, then the Lord will take me up.

My father hadn't forsaken me, but he was absent all through my teen years. I took that scripture to be the Lord speaking to me, saying He would be my dad and take care of me. I leaned on Him when I had problems and let Him fill the void.

Indeed, the Lord answered the prayer I prayed during my dad's funeral. God has revealed Himself to me and through me. Through this ministry and our Charis Bible College, He is touching the world, but that didn't just happen automatically. I had to choose to be better rather than bitter.

The point I am making is, if something negative happens in your life, you don't have to have a negative reaction. It is not predetermined. There is nothing physical that makes it that way. You can choose how you want to be.

Selfless Perspective

Only by pride cometh contention: but with the well advised is wisdom.

Proverbs 13:10

I once saw a program on television that was trying to persuade people to end the death penalty. They wanted life imprisonment to become the most severe form of judicial sentencing.

Now, I'm not excited about capital punishment, but I believe it is a biblically sound, sometimes appropriate means of deterring violent crime (Gen. 9:5–6). I'm firm in that conviction, but as I watched this program, I started to think about these things.

They told the story of a man who raped and murdered a young girl. But instead of focusing on the facts of the case, they began to weave a storyline together that started in this man's childhood. And it was emotional.

As I watched his baby pictures flash across the television screen, it was difficult to imagine that this innocent child could do anything worthy of death. I watched him grow up playing in the backyard, riding a stick horse, and climbing trees. Then I heard of the abuse he suffered as a child and how that trauma affected him. When they showed this man sitting in a dark cell with his head in his hands, I began to sympathize with him.

Though I knew what he did was wrong, I began to pity him. I thought, *Oh God, there are so many extenuating circumstances. Is there not a better way to deal with this man?* It made me question what I believed. But as I contemplated all this, the Lord spoke to my heart.

He said, "Andrew, what if they did a story on the girl this man raped and murdered? What if they showed her baby pictures? What if they showed her playing with dolls?" I got to thinking about that girl, who she was, and the calling God had put on her life. I also thought about the plans she may have had to get married and raise a family.

Then the Lord said, "What if, in the middle of all that, they told you that some pervert assaulted her for his own gratification, and then wasn't man enough to face what he'd done, so he killed her to cover up his crime?"

I saw that this man had made a choice. Instead of overcoming the abuse he suffered as a child, he turned the corner from victim to predator. In that moment, I realized that the exact same audience who was feeling sympathetic after seeing the man's side of the story would turn into a vigilante committee and string him up from the nearest tree when viewing things from the girl's viewpoint. The Lord spoke again, saying, "It all depends on which perspective you take. Your emotions will respond to either one."

This program used psychology to try and show that people shouldn't be accountable for their actions because something made them the way they are today. But the Bible says the only thing that causes anger, contention, and strife is pride—or looking at things only from a selfish viewpoint.

Be Dependent on God

Pride goeth before destruction, and an haughty spirit before a fall.

Proverbs 16:18

There was a man who, in the 1980s, may have had the largest ministry on earth at that time. He was on television and filling arenas, and people were giving millions of dollars a month to his ministry. But then he fell into sexual sin and destroyed everything he built. I remember watching the broadcast of this man's confession, and what he said really stuck with me.

This man said that, through television, he was reaching more people than Jesus did, which was probably true. But then, he said something that really knocked me back. This minister said he thought he could do anything. Ultimately, that was the problem that led to this man's sexual sin—he was lifted up in pride. He wasn't dependent on God anymore. He thought he was the one who caused all his success through some virtue of his own.

People like to claim the promise of Philippians 4:13, which says, *"I can do all things,"* but then they stop right there. They leave off the rest of the verse, which says, *"through Christ which strengtheneth me."* The moment you separate yourself from God and start believing your own press releases—when you no longer rely on Him as your source—you're headed for destruction.

It's like that man who thinks he can fly just because he's inside a plane, tens of thousands of feet above the ground. If he stepped out of that plane, how well do you think he could fly? It's only his position inside that plane that allows him to fly. Likewise, it's only our position in Christ that allows us to do anything (John 15:5).

I believe pride is also the root of what happened to David (2 Sam. 11:1–12:14). As long as David was fleeing from his father-in-law and in desperate straits, he was humble and trusted God. There really wasn't much else he could do. But when he was a very successful king, who had subdued all his foes, he took his eyes off the Lord and became self-confident.

As a result, while his army was out fighting the enemy, he spent his time at home, sleeping during the day, and getting up at night. In other words, David was bored. That's how he spied on Bathsheba bathing. David, a man after God's own heart, lusted after Bathsheba, had an affair with her, got her pregnant, and killed her husband Uriah to cover it up.

David no longer depended upon the Lord as he had in the past. His self-reliance was pride, and that was his downfall. You see, the middle letter of "p-r-i-d-e" is "I." At its core, pride is just being focused and reliant on yourself.

If at any point, you think, *Look at what I've done and how great I am*, you've just stepped out of God's goodness—and you will fall. Pride can cloud a person's judgment and allow them to be controlled by their own emotions and desires.

Sin Is Conceived

But every man is tempted, when he is drawn away of his own lust, and enticed. Then when lust hath conceived, it bringeth forth sin: and sin, when it is finished, bringeth forth death.

James 1:14–15

Sin is conceived in your emotions. That's a huge statement! Emotions are like your spiritual womb. Whatever emotions you allow to function on the inside of you are allowing seeds to be sown. And eventually, they are going to spring up.

You conceive when you express emotions. If you are rejoicing and praising God, you are conceiving good things that are eventually going to come to birth in your life. If you have negative emotions, you are conceiving evil things.

When you are depressed, bitter, or expressing some other negative emotion, it is like having spiritual intercourse with the devil. You are allowing Satan to impregnate you with something. I hope this isn't offensive to you, but this is the logic of these verses.

The only way you're going to avoid the birth of negative things is to somehow terminate the pregnancy. And that's not the way to control birth! You don't just indulge yourself, conceive something, and then abort it so that you don't have to live with the consequences.

I know that may seem really strong, but I'm trying to illustrate a point. I don't think most people think this way, because if they did, they probably wouldn't give Satan access to their lives. The best way to avoid a birth is to avoid the conception.

Most people would not say, "Alright Satan, plant your thoughts of suicide and other negative things in my life. Just do your worst." But when something negative happens, negative feelings come with it, and they'll just allow their emotions to run rampant—not thinking about what the consequences might be.

There are people who attempt or commit suicide, but they don't really want to do it. They may tell people, "I can't help the way I feel," but the truth is they couldn't have even considered suicide unless they had first indulged depression, discouragement, and other negative emotions. Those seeds of suicide are planted in a person in their emotions, and they eventually act it out with deadly consequences.

When you allow discouragement to get inside you and don't counter it with something positive like rejoicing, you are allowing Satan to plant seeds in you—in your emotions. It's up to you to stop the conception before it starts.

Let Not Your Heart Be Troubled

Let not your heart be troubled: ye believe in God, believe also in me.

John 14:1

It's important that you understand the context of this. Jesus spoke this to His disciples the night before His crucifixion. Jesus told His disciples not to let their hearts be troubled *right before* He went to the Garden of Gethsemane and prayed, was betrayed and arrested, taken to a mock trial, and sent to die on the cross. All those things were just hours away when Jesus said these things.

You have to remember that these disciples had left everything. They had fishing boats, businesses, and families, and they left these things behind to follow Jesus. They hinged everything on the fact that Jesus was the Messiah. And if you read on in John 14, you'll see the disciples didn't remember the scriptures about Jesus being raised from the dead. Even though he had prophesied these things, they were shocked and amazed when He was resurrected.

The period between Jesus' crucifixion and resurrection was going to be a bleak time. It looked like all the disciples' hope and faith in Jesus was misplaced. I'm sure they were tempted to think He was only a man whom the Romans and Jewish leaders overcame. They didn't understand that it was a part of God's plan—that Jesus had to shed His blood, go redeem the souls that were in hell, and bring them to heaven.

Jesus was going to be beaten and crucified in agony, yet He told His disciples, "Don't let your hearts be troubled." Psychology would lead people to think, *That's unreasonable. That's wrong. You're telling people to suppress their feelings. They should be grieving. They should be brokenhearted.*

Psychology has taught people that if you don't vent, let it all out, and give in to your emotions, you're in denial. People are taught that they're actually doing damage if they suppress and hold things in. Well, there may be some partial truth in that, but there are certain things that you should never vent or give in to. We should cast all our care upon the Lord instead of holding it in (1 Pet. 5:7).

The Bible teaches us that we have authority and can control our emotions. When Jesus spoke these things to His disciples, He did so in the second-person imperative. In other words, the implied subject of His instructions was "you." That means the power and authority to control your feelings rest upon *you!*

You may be thinking, *But you just don't know what I'm going through!* Maybe I don't, and I'm not trying to dismiss your situation, but what you are going through is nothing like what Jesus' disciples went through between His crucifixion and resurrection. And yet, Jesus told them, *"Let not your heart be troubled."*

Bringing Power Under Authority

I've had horses nearly my entire life. I've learned that if a person ever lets go of a horse and it gets out of control, it's nearly impossible to ever regain control.

If you let a horse get up a full head of steam, and it's not under control, you are going to wind up in trouble. The best thing for you to do in that situation is just jump off that horse and hope you land someplace soft. Even though I had relatively small horses (Arabians), they were still around 1,100 pounds. So, it's hard to bring something with that much muscle and strength under control once it builds up momentum.

A horse is a powerful animal. Anything powerful has the potential for good, but it also has the potential for bad. Nuclear energy can be used to make an atomic bomb that will destroy a city, or it can be used to generate electricity and do positive things. Things that are powerful have to be harnessed and used correctly. In the same way, emotions are powerful, and they need to be harnessed to produce positive things in your life.

My horses were what they call "green broke." That's because I wouldn't ride them but once or twice every month. I just didn't spend that much time working with them. So, a person could ride them, but these horses tended to do things they just shouldn't do.

Years ago, a friend of mine brought his seven-year-old son over to ride one of my horses. So, I taught this young boy how to keep the horse from running off and how to control it using a bit—the metal piece in the horse's mouth used for steering.

He rode a horse that was green broke for two and a half hours and didn't have a single problem because he just followed my instructions and controlled an animal that weighed more than 1,000 pounds.

A few hours later, I had another guy come out who was in his mid-twenties—he was a grown man. He had just been married and had his wife with him. I started to give this man some of the same instructions that I'd given that seven-year-old boy, but he didn't want to hear it. He was trying to impress his new bride and said, "Oh, I can ride this horse. No problem!"

Wouldn't you know, in just a few minutes, that horse had thrown this full-grown man into a barbed wire fence and sent him to the hospital. It was all because that man didn't follow my instructions.

It was the exact same horse on the exact same day. But the difference was that one person was in control and knew what to do, while the other person didn't use the power and authority he had. That horse knew the grown man wasn't really going to take control over him, so it took advantage. It's the same way with a person's emotions.

Exercising Control

Behold, we put bits in the horses' mouths, that they may obey us; and we turn about their whole body.

James 3:3

When a person puts a bit and a bridle in a horse's mouth, they can "*turn about their whole body.*" Compared to the size of a horse, the bit and bridle are relatively small things. And yet you can control a horse with them.

James said your tongue is like a bit and bridle. Your words can control your whole body. They can control your actions. That's how powerful words are. But in making that comparison, James talked about how a person can turn a horse's whole body around, just with a bit in their mouth.

You see, God created the horse so that it can't do anything without using its head. If you've ever seen a horse lying on the ground, it has to throw its head up before it can get up. That means you could step on its head, put some pressure on it, and a huge animal that may weigh five to ten times more than an average person wouldn't be able to get up off the ground.

Likewise, if a horse is up, it can't get down on the ground unless it puts its head down first. I once had a horse that didn't like people riding it. Again, I didn't ride my horses often enough to ever get them totally broke the way they should be, so it was always exciting to ride!

That horse would just get tired of riding, lie down on the ground, and start rolling to try to get a person off its back. That can be a dangerous situation. But I had learned that under normal circumstances, a horse cannot get down unless it puts its head down first. So, anytime that horse would start to put its head down, I'd just pull its head back up using the bridle, and it could not get down and roll. If I just paid attention to what the horse would do, I could stop it before it started.

In a similar way, a horse cannot run straight if his head is pointed to the side. It will go in the direction of its head. So, before a horse gets out of control and starts to run, you can take just one rein and pull it to the side. Then, when the horse feels the pressure on its bit, it will obey. If you turn that horse's head to the side, it'll turn, go in a circle, and eventually stop.

Now, I realize doing these things may not be the best way to train horses, and I'm not an expert horseman, but the Lord has shown me to control—or harness—my emotions the same way I would work with my horses. What I am saying is that a person has to observe and take charge of their emotions before they get out of control and someone gets hurt!

A Merry Heart Does Good

A merry heart doeth good like *a medicine: but a broken spirit drieth the bones.*

Proverbs 17:22

Now, if you've never been around horses, you may not relate to these things. But I think it's a perfect illustration that if you ever let your emotions go—if you give in to grief, unforgiveness, and other negative emotions—the damage that is done is nearly irreparable.

For example, if you get angry at somebody, it just seems to affect everything. It affects the relationship. It can affect the way you sleep. It can even affect your health.

There are medical professionals who will tell you that when you're under stress and depression, those things suppress your immune system. Your negative emotions can make you more susceptible to certain things. I've heard that some studies link your emotional state to whether you can overcome diseases.

I remember a lady who thought she was pregnant but found out she had cancer instead. The doctors said she needed a hysterectomy immediately. They said she only had a 50 percent chance of living, and she wouldn't live more than two weeks without surgery.

She came to me, crying, "Andrew, have you heard what they said?" You could hear the worry in her voice. I started laughing and said, "Cancer's no problem with God. The lights in heaven won't dim from the power drain if the Lord heals you! It's not any harder to be healed of cancer than it is to be healed of a cold."

Now, I don't always respond that way, but I believed the Lord was leading me to show a positive attitude, and it really got her attention!

The only thing that made the cancer seem insurmountable was the value she placed on what the doctors said. In the end, that woman decided to stand her ground and believe God for healing. She overcame that cancer and went on to have a whole slew of children. Having joy and peace is healthy; it's beneficial to you.

In our health-crazed Christian world today, much is made of diet and exercise, but very little is made of having a merry heart. This is just my opinion, but I suspect that food and exercise account for less than twenty percent of your total health. That is not to say that we don't need to eat right and exercise, but having a merry heart is so much more important. There are spiritual factors that are far more important to the quality and length of your life.

Years ago, I heard about a man who received a serious diagnosis, and rather than just rely on conventional medicine, he decided to follow the old adage that "laughter is the best medicine." He was a medical doctor and knew that people with his diagnosis had a very slim chance of survival. He decided to watch old slapstick comedy movies that made him laugh. Instead of getting down and depressed about his diagnosis, he decided to keep a positive attitude.

Even though his doctors were skeptical, this man recovered from the disease, wrote a couple of books about his experience, and eventually taught in a major medical school about the connection between emotions and physical health.[2] In other words, he demonstrated that "*a merry heart doeth good* like *a medicine*" (Prov. 17:22).

How Do You See Yourself?

And there we saw the giants, the sons of Anak, which come of the giants: and we were in our own sight as grasshoppers, and so we were in their sight.

Numbers 13:33

We think in pictures. For example, if I said "dog," you probably wouldn't think of the letters "d-o-g" written on a page. You would think of the animal, and likely one you've owned. With each added word—"black dog," "big, black dog," or "big, black, mean dog"—the perception in your mind changes.

Similarly, each one of us has a picture of ourselves. It's like a snapshot of who we are. That inward picture determines the way we act and react to things on the outside. In this case, the Israelites saw themselves as grasshoppers in comparison to the inhabitants of the Promised Land. As a result, they were afraid to go in and possess what God had provided for them.

If you see yourself as weak and incompetent, you will have no confidence. If you see yourself as an angry, violent person, you will react to stress accordingly. The mental image you have of yourself will dictate your response when a challenge comes your way.

But when you make Jesus your Lord (Rom. 10:9), you become a brand-new person (2 Cor. 5:17). You have to see yourself in Christ, in the spirit, as a new creation. Seeing yourself that way will totally change your reactions.

Years ago, when I was pastoring, I had a guy come to me talking about the division he saw in our church. I said, "Yes, there are problems, but you're the source of it! We didn't have all these problems before you came here." That caught this guy off guard, and I thought he was going to get really mad, but instead, he just opened up to me.

This man, who was causing all kinds of problems in the church, told me he was indicted by a grand jury three times before he was thirteen years old. He grew up in reformatories and foster homes. He said, "I don't know what normal is. Strife is normal for me."

He told me that there were a lot of things he knew about. As a matter of fact, he often had something to say to everyone because he wanted people to view him as an expert on certain things. But then he said, "If you asked me how to love, I wouldn't really know how, because I've never experienced it."

This man's life was so full of strife and bitterness that one time when I went to his house, I found him beating on a car with a two-by-four piece of lumber and yelling all kinds of curse words. When he saw me, of course, he changed his tune and became apologetic. But this man only saw his life as full of strife, and he acted accordingly.

That really enlightened me because I grew up in a home where we loved each other. But there are some people whose idea of normal is totally perverted. Sad to say, there's so much strife and division in our society today that we just accept it as normal. When people's emotions get out of control and their anger boils over, we don't even think about it.

Change Your Thinking

That ye put off concerning the former conversation the old man, which is corrupt according to the deceitful lusts; and be renewed in the spirit of your mind; and that ye put on the new man, which after God is created in righteousness and true holiness.

Ephesians 4:22–24

Here, the Apostle Paul says to be "*renewed in the spirit of your mind.*" The *New International Version* says to be "*made new in the attitude of your minds.*" The *Amplified Bible* says to have "*a fresh mental and spiritual attitude.*" So, this is not just talking about *what* we think but also the *way* we think—our attitudes and entire outlook on life.

For instance, pessimism is an attitude just as optimism is an attitude. Given the same facts, a pessimist and an optimist will think totally differently about the same situation. They have programmed themselves to respond differently to those facts. A pessimist will look at a situation and focus on the negative side of it, while an optimist will look at the same situation and focus on the positive side.

The word "*spirit*" in verse 23 is not talking about the Holy Spirit or even the born-again spirit. It is speaking of our attitude. The Greek word *pneuma*, which was translated "*spirit*" here, can mean "mental disposition."[3] That's the way it is used here. Paul was saying that we not only have to reprogram our minds with new information, but also allow these new truths to change our attitudes.

Many people have been taught biblical truths but often don't meditate on them to the degree that those truths change their attitudes. For instance, they can know that it's God's will that they prosper financially, but if they don't start seeing themselves with their needs met, their attitude hasn't changed. A poverty attitude will cause them to stay poor even though they know God wants them to prosper.

It's not good enough to just learn truths from God's Word. We have to meditate on them until our own thinking has been renewed to God's way of thinking.

To harness our emotions, we must change the way we think. We have got to recognize that with Jesus Christ on our side, we now have a supernatural ability. This is something we didn't have before we came to know Him as Savior and Lord. We need to quit comparing ourselves with the world, expecting the same results the world expects, because they do not have God actively involved in their lives.

God wants to be involved in everyone's life. To most people, He is on the outside. But as believers, He now lives on the inside of us. God deposited His life and supernatural ability on the inside of us; therefore, there needs to be an entire attitude change within us. As our attitude changes, our emotions follow along and change with it. Our emotions are one hundred percent influenced by our thoughts and how we think.

Renew Your Mind

I beseech you therefore, brethren, by the mercies of God, that ye present your bodies a living sacrifice, holy, acceptable unto God, which is *your reasonable service. And be*

> *not conformed to this world: but be ye transformed by the renewing of your mind, that ye may prove what is that good, and acceptable, and perfect, will of God.*
>
> Romans 12:1-2

In our born-again spirits, we have everything we need to live the victorious Christian life. So, why are Christians letting their emotions get out of control? It's because they haven't renewed their minds.

According to Romans 12:1, the first step in serving God is the giving of our entire selves to the Lord. But the second verse goes on to say that we must not be conformed to this world. I like to say, "Don't be poured into the world's mold." So, we spend the rest of our lives renewing our minds to God's Word.

The Greek word translated as "*transformed*" in this verse is *metamorphoo*, which is the root of the word "metamorphosis."[4] This is the process that takes place when a caterpillar spins a cocoon, lives in it, and is transformed into a butterfly.

To have that kind of transformation take place in your emotions and your actions, you must renew your mind. Go through the New Testament and read and meditate on all the scriptures that describe who you are in Christ.

When you do this, acknowledge that when you made Jesus Christ the Lord of your life, you were born again. You don't just get a new start or a new beginning, you have an entirely new life.

There is a totally new person on the inside of you in your spirit (2 Cor. 5:17).

Then, develop a mental picture of who you are in Christ. As you think in your heart, that's the way you are going to be (Prov. 23:7). If you don't see yourself as a new person, you will revert to your old ways of thinking and be dominated by your emotions.

But if you can begin seeing yourself as a brand-new person in Christ, you will begin to emotionally feel and physically act like a victor rather than a victim. This is because the Word of God is a mirror of who you really are (James 1:23). Meditating on the Word produces a mindset that will be reproduced in your lifestyle.

If you are defeated, angry, bitter, depressed, or lonely, it's because you see yourself that way. You are seeing yourself in light of your problems. You are looking at failure and receiving what you see. But if you can begin to see who you are in Christ, then you can begin to reproduce that image in your actions and your emotions and find hope for today and tomorrow.

Our Light Afflictions

For our light affliction, which is but for a moment, worketh for us a far more exceeding and eternal weight of glory.

2 Corinthians 4:17

When you are following God's call on your life, you may feel like there is a huge target painted on your back because Satan is going to attack you! But you can overcome if you operate in what the Word of God says.

When the Apostle Paul wrote this verse, he wasn't saying that he was defeated. He had problems, but he said they were just a *"light affliction."* It was all in the way he evaluated things and harnessed his emotions. It was his relationship—eternal life (John 17:3)—with God that helped Paul process the things that happened to him. It reduced these situations to their correct proportion in relation to God.

In contrast, some of you have made huge problems out of things that aren't that big of a deal. Now, I'm not saying that some people aren't facing major financial, emotional, and relational problems. I'm not trying to minimize those things, but I am saying that there are many people who make big problems out of things that are relatively small.

As a matter of fact, there are times when people share with me some of the things they think are such a big deal. I have to bite my lip to keep from laughing. That's because I've had a lot of negative things happen to me over the years. I've been criticized and maligned. I've been lied about. I've even been kidnapped!

But someday, when I've been in the presence of the Lord for 10,000 years (as the song "Amazing Grace" says), will the things I'm facing today really matter? Are they really that big of a deal in the light of eternity?

Let me share with you some of the things that Paul called light afflictions. He was beaten with rods and whips multiple times, stoned, left for dead, imprisoned, and shipwrecked (2 Cor. 11:23–30). When Paul went to a town, instead of checking in to a hotel, he probably just stopped by the prison and said, "Save a spot for me because I'll be back!" He suffered hunger, cold, nakedness, and everything mentioned above—all for the sake of the Gospel.

Paul was so excited about the revelation of the Lord on the inside that all the things he suffered on the outside seemed like nothing in comparison. He didn't ignore the fact that he had problems in this life; he just didn't focus on them. Paul was able to look at his life in light of eternity, and in that light, his afflictions were just for a moment.

If we would learn to think that way, it would shrink our problems to their actual proportion, and our emotions would not get out of control as a result.

Rejoice in the Lord

Rejoice in the Lord alway: and *again I say, Rejoice.*

Philippians 4:4

I believe the reason Paul repeated himself here is that when he said, *"Rejoice in the Lord alway,"* people probably thought,

Well, he can't mean always. So, he continued, *"again I say, Rejoice."* He emphasized that we are supposed to rejoice in the Lord always. And if you look that word up in the Greek, it means "always."[5]

When Paul says to rejoice, it is a command, not an option. It doesn't say to rejoice if we feel like it, if we are in the mood, or if everything is going our way. I can say right now that most times, we won't feel like rejoicing. Most times, we won't be in the mood. And most times, everything won't be going our way. However, we are still commanded to rejoice in the Lord at all times. God would not give us a command we could not fulfill.

Those who don't follow this command are resisting the Word of God just as much as those who don't follow some of the moral laws, such as not stealing or committing adultery. This is a law of the Lord, and it removes any doubt we may have about not having authority over our emotions.

If emotions were only uncontrollable psychological reactions to circumstances, then the Lord would be unjust to give us an impossible command and then hold us accountable (Deut. 28:47–48). But God is not unjust, and we are commanded to rejoice always. Therefore, we can and should control our emotions.

You can control your emotions. You are not just an animal. You can choose how to respond in a crisis situation.

When Paul and Silas were thrown in prison (Acts 16:16–24), I guarantee you it didn't produce good feelings in their flesh.

But they were so in love with God, they just rejoiced in spite of their situation.

> *And at midnight Paul and Silas prayed, and sang praises unto God: and the prisoners heard them.*
>
> Acts 16:25

They were praising God so joyfully that the other prisoners *"heard them."* If you look this up in the Greek, it means they gave "rapt attention" to what Paul and Silas were singing.[6] The prisoners weren't just listening with their physical ears; they were listening with their hearts. Paul and Silas' praise ministered to the prisoners.

The prisoners were so blessed by Paul and Silas that none of them left when an earthquake came, the prison doors were opened, and all of their chains fell off. And what's more, their jailer received the Gospel and was saved! You see, Paul and Silas chose to rejoice in the Lord in prison, and they ended up ministering to others as a result. Now, when was the last time your praise in a terrible situation ministered to someone?

Bless the Lord at All Times

On March 4, 2001, I received a call at 4:05 a.m. from my oldest son telling me that my youngest son was dead. He had been dead for over four hours. They had placed him in a morgue, in a cooler, with a toe tag on.

Now, what would happen if you woke up in the middle of the night and someone told you that your child was dead? What would you feel? Well, I can guarantee you, I felt everything that anybody else would feel.

I had every emotion of grief and sorrow that you could imagine. I don't deny that is how I felt. But I also knew Jesus bore my grief and carried my sorrow (Is. 53:4). I had renewed my mind to that truth, and I didn't have to let my emotions control me. So, before I hung up the phone, I said, "Don't let anybody touch him until I get there. The first report is not the last report!"

Jamie and I prayed, and we called our son back to life. But if I hadn't known what the Word says about the Lord being a good God (John 10:10), I could have let emotions overwhelm me. I could have even felt anger and bitterness toward God, and asked questions like, "Why did You let this happen?" But praise God, I knew He didn't cause or let it happen.

Instead, I began to take my authority. I started praising God. I quoted scriptures like Psalm 34:1, which says,

I will bless the Lord *at all times: his praise* shall *continually* be *in my mouth.*

I praised God out loud and thanked Him for His comfort and power. That's not how I felt, but that's what I believed.

When I did that, the Spirit of God rose up inside me, and my faith revived. The Lord spoke things to me that assured me my son would live again. I had the *"peace of God, which passeth all understanding"* (Phil. 4:7). As a matter of fact, I told my wife that this was going to be the greatest miracle we had ever seen!

Sure enough, when we got to the hospital, my oldest son greeted me and told me that my youngest son sat up and started talking a few minutes after he called. There was no brain damage, even though he had been dead between four and five hours. It was a miracle that would not have happened if I had been controlled by my emotions. Praise the Lord!

You Can Control Your Emotions

Just like I did in that crisis situation, you can control your emotions. The Scriptures clearly reveal that our actions are the result of how we think (Prov. 23:7), not just a by-product of what happens to us. But most people are convinced they can't control their thinking and therefore can't control their emotions. If something bad happens, what choice do we have but to be hurt, angry, or discouraged? But that's not what Paul taught.

Paul said we have the mind of Christ (1 Cor. 2:16). He also told us to let that same mind be in us as it was in Christ (Phil. 2:5). Furthermore, Paul also said we are to arm ourselves with the same mind that Christ had (1 Pet. 4:1).

Do you think Jesus would be thinking and feeling the way you are? Can you see Jesus reacting to your problems the way you do? I dare to say each one of us would have to admit we don't think like Jesus would in our situation. But then most of us would say, "I'm not Jesus! I just can't help it!" That's not what 2 Cor. 10:4-5 says:

(For the weapons of our warfare are not carnal, but mighty through God to the pulling down of strong holds;) Casting down imaginations, and every high thing that exalteth itself against the knowledge of God, and bringing into captivity every thought to the obedience of Christ.

Paul said the Lord has given us such powerful weapons that we can bring *every* thought into captivity and under obedience to Christ. If our mind is stayed upon Christ, with every thought under the captivity and obedience to God's Word, then we will have perfect peace (Is. 26:3).

Paul also revealed that our new, born-again spirits already have love, joy, peace, longsuffering, gentleness, goodness, faith, meekness, and temperance (Gal. 5:22-23). These aren't emotions we can receive if we do everything right. These are realities that already exist in the spirit of everyone who has made Jesus the Lord of their lives. So, when we lack any of these qualities, we aren't drawing on our new life in Christ. We are living out of what the Bible calls our flesh, which refers to our mind and emotions.

The key to victorious living is walking in these realities that already exist in our spirits instead of letting our mind and emotions control us (Gal. 5:16). Anytime we experience the negative emotions of hate, depression, anxiety, impatience, harshness, badness, fear, pride, and lack of self-control, we are letting the flesh dominate us. The antidote is to walk in our new, born-again spirits that have all these positive fruit of the Spirit.

When I pastored in Pritchett, Colorado, I had a lot of opposition. I left a successful church in Texas to come and pastor a group of ten people in Pritchett, a town of 144 people. In six months, we grew to one hundred in attendance, but the original members resented it. They wanted to keep the church small, with just the few friends they always had. They accused me of every sin in the book. It started taking a toll on me.

One night, I was determined to just let my emotions go and give in to a pity party. I had sent out invitations to every demon in that county, and I was just waiting for Jamie and my boys to go to sleep so I could go down into the basement and start complaining. While I was waiting, I just flopped my Bible open, and it landed on Galatians 5:22-23.

Now I don't recommend that method of Bible study, but desperate times call for desperate measures. The Lord mercifully brought me to these very scriptures that I knew so well. I knew what He was saying to me, but I didn't want to hear it. I thought I would feel so much better if I just vented and let all my unbelief out. But that's not walking in the spirit. That would be indulging my flesh, and I would conceive something I didn't want to give birth to.

Praise the Lord, I made the right decision, and by the time I went down into the basement, I started praising the Lord. I didn't feel like it at first. I was praising the Lord totally by faith through gritted teeth, but I did it. I was acting on what the Bible said I had in my spirit and not what I felt in my flesh.

In just a few minutes, I began drawing out the love, joy, and peace that were in my spirit. I wound up having a tremendous time of worship and thanksgiving, and my emotions got in line and under my control. I don't know what would have happened if I had just let go and embraced the depression that was knocking at my door, but I know it wouldn't have been good. It's possible that might have been the end of my ministry. It sure felt like it.

Conclusion

We were created with emotions and have been given the power through Jesus Christ to control them. We must accept that responsibility and learn how to properly release those emotions.

The answer to harnessing our emotions is not found in the world's psychology but rather by choosing to apply the Word of

God in faith. If we look at our circumstances and situations in the light of eternity, we will see they are only for a moment. We are more than conquerors over everything the world throws our way, and we need to begin seeing ourselves that way.

Psychology tries to help us develop a good self-image to make us feel good about ourselves. But that is not the answer. Self will ultimately fail. We are to find our Christ-esteem in what Jesus has done and what has already been placed in our born-again spirits.

Renew your mind according to the Word of God and identify with who you are in Christ. Esteem Him on the inside of you and recognize that He has given you control over your emotions. When you take control and harness your emotions, you can then live in peace of mind and heart, rejoicing with joy unspeakable and full of glory.

FURTHER STUDY

If you enjoyed this booklet and would like to learn more about some of the things I've shared, I suggest my teachings:

1. *Spirit, Soul & Body*
2. *Jesus' Farewell Address*
3. *Effortless Change*
4. *Hardness of Heart*
5. *Self-Centeredness: The Source of All Grief*
6. *The Power of Praise*

Plus 200,000 hours of free teaching on our website at **awmi.net**.

Additional resources are available for purchase at **awmi.net/store**.

Go deeper in your relationship with God by browsing all of Andrew's free teachings.

Receive Jesus as Your Savior

Choosing to receive Jesus Christ as your Lord and Savior is the most important decision you'll ever make!

God's Word promises, *"That if thou shalt confess with thy mouth the Lord Jesus, and shalt believe in thine heart that God hath raised him from the dead, thou shalt be saved. For with the heart man believeth unto righteousness; and with the mouth confession is made unto salvation"* (Rom. 10:9–10). *"For whosoever shall call upon the name of the Lord shall be saved"* (Rom. 10:13). By His grace, God has already done everything to provide salvation. Your part is simply to believe and receive.

Pray out loud: "Jesus, I confess that You are my Lord and Savior. I believe in my heart that God raised You from the dead. By faith in Your Word, I receive salvation now. Thank You for saving me."

The very moment you commit your life to Jesus Christ, the truth of His Word instantly comes to pass in your spirit. Now that you're born again, there's a brand-new you!

Please contact us and let us know that you've prayed to receive Jesus as your Savior. We'd like to send you some free materials to help you on your new journey. Call our Helpline:

719-635-1111 (available 24 hours a day, seven days a week) to speak to a staff member who is here to help you understand and grow in your new relationship with the Lord.

Welcome to your new life!

Receive the Holy Spirit

As His child, your loving heavenly Father wants to give you the supernatural power you need to live a new life. *"For every one that asketh receiveth; and he that seeketh findeth; and to him that knocketh it shall be opened…how much more shall* your *heavenly Father give the Holy Spirit to them that ask him?"* (Luke 11:10–13).

All you have to do is ask, believe, and receive!

Pray this: "Father, I recognize my need for Your power to live a new life. Please fill me with Your Holy Spirit. By faith, I receive it right now. Thank You for baptizing me. Holy Spirit, You are welcome in my life."

Some syllables from a language you don't recognize will rise up from your heart to your mouth (1 Cor. 14:14). As you speak them out loud by faith, you're releasing God's power from within and building yourself up in the spirit (1 Cor. 14:4). You can do this whenever and wherever you like.

It doesn't really matter whether you felt anything or not when you prayed to receive the Lord and His Spirit. If you believed in your heart that you received, then God's Word promises you did. *"Therefore I say unto you, What things soever ye desire, when ye pray, believe that ye receive* them, *and ye shall have* them*"* (Mark 11:24). God always honors His Word—believe it!

We would like to rejoice with you and help you understand more fully what has taken place in your life!

Please contact us to let us know that you've prayed to be filled with the Holy Spirit and to request the book *The New You & the Holy Spirit*. This book will explain in more detail about the benefits of being filled with the Holy Spirit and speaking in tongues. Call our Helpline: **719-635-1111** (available 24 hours a day, seven days a week).

Call for Prayer

If you need prayer for any reason, you can call our Helpline, 24 hours a day, seven days a week at **719-635-1111**. A trained prayer minister will answer your call and pray with you.

Every day, we receive testimonies of healings and other miracles from our Helpline, and we are ministering God's nearly-too-good-to-be-true message of the Gospel to more people than ever. So, I encourage you to call today!

Endnotes

1. *Blue Letter Bible*, s.v. "ψυχή" ("psychē"), accessed June 6, 2024, https://www.blueletterbible.org/lexicon/g5590/kjv/tr/0-1/

2. Dan Gordon, "Laughing All the Way," *UCLA Magazine*, July 1, 2019, https://newsroom.ucla.edu/magazine/norman-cousins-humor-health-mind-body.

3. *Strong's Definitions*, s.v. "πνεῦμα" ("pneuma"), accessed June 20, 2024, https://www.blueletterbible.org/lexicon/g4151/kjv/tr/0-1/

4. *Blue Letter Bible*, s.v. "μεταμορφόω" ("metamorphoō"), accessed June 17, 2024, https://www.blueletterbible.org/lexicon/g3339/kjv/tr/0-1/

5. *Thayer's Greek Lexicon*, s.v. "πάντοτε" ("pantote"), accessed June 20, 2024, https://www.blueletterbible.org/lexicon/g3842/kjv/tr/0-1/

6. *Vine's Expository Dictionary of New Testament Words*, s.v., "ἐπακροάομαι" ("epakroaomai"), accessed June 20, 2024, https://www.blueletterbible.org/lexicon/g1874/kjv/tr/0-1/

About the Author

Andrew Wommack's life was forever changed the moment he encountered the supernatural love of God on March 23, 1968. As a renowned Bible teacher and author, Andrew has made it his mission to change the way the world sees God.

Andrew's vision is to go as far and deep with the Gospel as possible. His message goes far through the *Gospel Truth* television program, which is available to over half the world's population. The message goes deep through discipleship at Charis Bible College, headquartered in Woodland Park, Colorado. Founded in 1994, Charis has campuses across the United States and around the globe.

Andrew also has an extensive library of teaching materials in print, audio, and video. More than 200,000 hours of free teachings can be accessed at **awmi.net**.

Contact Information

Andrew Wommack Ministries, Inc.
PO Box 3333
Colorado Springs, CO 80934-3333
info@awmi.net
awmi.net
Helpline: 719-635-1111 (available 24/7)

Charis Bible College
info@charisbiblecollege.org
844-360-9577
CharisBibleCollege.org

For a complete list of our offices, visit
awmi.net/contact-us.

Connect with us on social media.

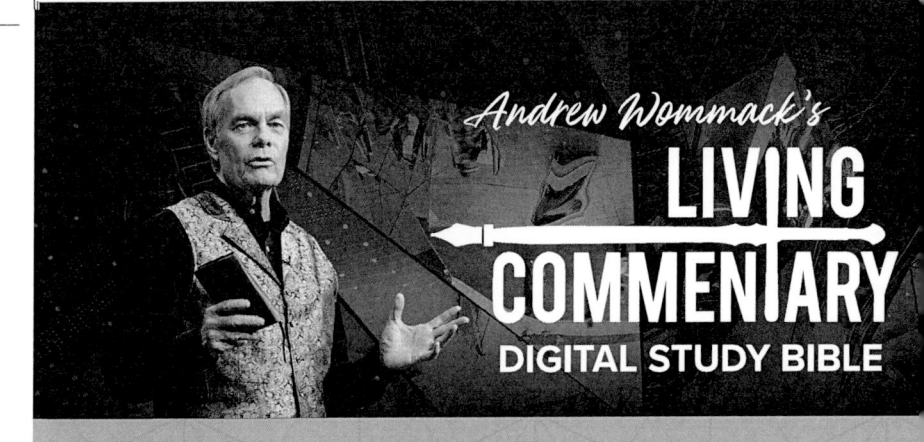

Andrew Wommack's LIVING COMMENTARY DIGITAL STUDY BIBLE

Andrew Wommack's *Living Commentary* digital study Bible is a user-friendly, downloadable program. It's like reading the Bible with Andrew at your side, sharing his revelation with you verse by verse.

Main features:
- Bible study software with a grace-and-faith perspective
- Over 27,000 notes by Andrew on verses from Genesis through Revelation
- *Adam Clarke's Commentary on the Bible*
- *Albert Barnes' Notes on the Whole Bible*
- *Matthew Henry's Concise Commentary*
- 12 Bible versions
- 3 optional premium translation add-ons: *New Living Translation*, *New International Version*, and *The Message* (additional purchase of $9.99 each)
- 2 concordances: *Englishman's Concordance* and *Strong's Concordance*
- 2 dictionaries: *Collaborative International Dictionary* and *Holman's Dictionary*
- Atlas with biblical maps
- Bible and *Living Commentary* statistics
- Quick navigation, including history of verses
- Robust search capabilities (for the Bible and Andrew's notes)
- "Living" (i.e., constantly updated and expanding)
- Ability to create personal notes
- Accessible online and offline

Whether you're new to studying the Bible or a seasoned Bible scholar, you'll gain a deeper revelation of the Word from a grace-and-faith perspective.

Purchase Andrew's *Living Commentary* today at **awmi.net/living** and grow in the Word with Andrew.

Item code: 8350

ANDREW WOMMACK MINISTRIES

Sign up to watch anytime, anywhere, for free.

GOSPEL TRUTH
NETWORK

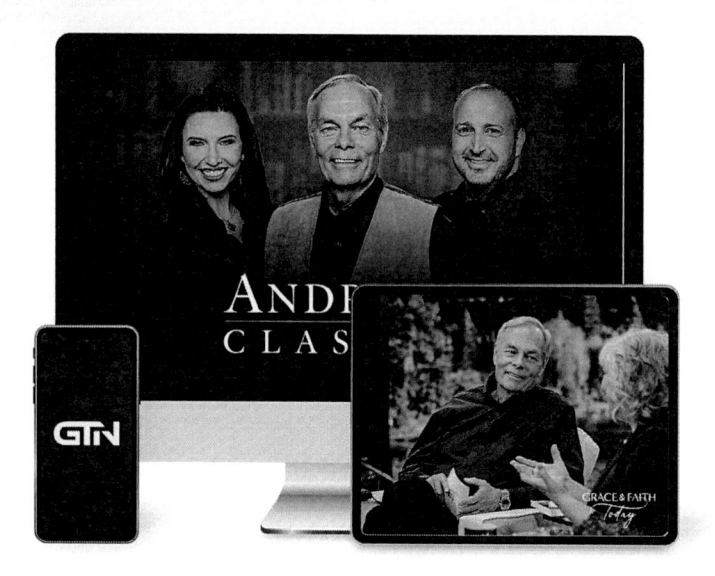

GTNTV.com

Download our apps available on mobile and TV platforms or stream GTN on Glorystar Satellite Network.